Sud Aviation SE.210 **CARAVELLE**
Timelines

Matt Falcus

A Royal Air Maroc Caravelle III sits on the ramp at Amsterdam Schiphol. The clean lines, rear-mounted engines and early T-tail were all attributes which the French airliner was known for, inspiring many later designs from other manufacturers.

First Edition 2023

ISBN 978 1 7398194 8 4

© 2023 Matthew Falcus
British Library Cataloguing-in-Publication Data
A catalogue record for this book is available from the British Library.
Published by Destinworld Publishing Ltd.
www.destinworld.com
Printed in India

Contents

About This Book

This book is intended as a pictorial history of the Sud Aviation SE.210 Caravelle, as seen through time in many of the liveries and operators it flew with. This is not an exhaustive history depicting every operator and airframe, though we have included information on the aircraft's development as well as surviving airframes.

For aviation enthusiasts, modellers and fans of classic airliners, I hope it provides a welcome addition to your bookshelf, a useful guide to the Caravelle, and a pleasing trip down memory lane.

Introduction

The end of the Second World War heralded a period in commercial aviation which had never be experienced before and, arguably, will never be repeated.

Years of conflict had stymied commercial air travel whilst, at the same time, had necessitated huge advances in technology surrounding aircraft development. As a result, a returning demand for air travel came at a time when aircraft manufacturers, airlines and governments would begin to push for new aircraft types offering the latest advances in technology and capabilities.

The United States, whose largest aircraft manufacturers, Boeing, Douglas and Lockheed, had benefitted from their 1930s and early 1940s designs being used heavily during the war were naturally inclined to continue pushing these types for airline use afterwards. The Douglas DC-4 and DC-6, and Lockheed Constellation in particular had not yet seen their full potential and were quickly pressed into further airline service.

Towards the end of the war advancements in jet engine technology had been proven in military aircraft and, as a result, Europe's aircraft manufacturers took the opportunity to develop this idea in passenger aircraft, most notably with the de Havilland Comet.

Boeing and Douglas soon responded with their own jet airliners, but these were targeted at long-range travel. Other manufacturers chose to focus on turboprop technology as a closer link to the older piston power known so well.

Like Britain, with its Brabazon Committee tasked with planning the country's output of new airliner designs, France began the 1950s with its own interest in developing home-grown airliners. Various manufacturers were already looking into new designs, but when the government run Direction Technique et Industrielle issued a specification for a new French airliner on November 6, 1951, it gave these manufacturers an outcome to focus on.

No powerplant was specified for the new type, but it was required to offer a 6,500kg (14,000lb) payload, capable of accommodating 55 to 65 passengers, and 1,00kg (2,000lb) of cargo. It must fly at speeds of 600kmh (325 knots) and have a range of 2,000km (1,240 miles), and be able to operate from 2,000m (6,560ft) runways.

Simultaneously it was known that various engine manufacturers were working on aircraft powerplants, and French manufacturers including Bréguet, Hurel-Dubois, SNCA du Nord and SNCA du Sud-Ouest all worked on their own jet and turboprop designs utilising these options.

SNCASE, or Société Nationale de Construction Aéronautique du Sud-Est, a study of the existing jet and turboprop options available in Britain and the United States, as well as the long-established piston market, led them to what they considered the best option: a medium-range jetliner targeted at airlines in Europe, the Middle

East and North Africa. At the time, no such aircraft was available, with the current crop of jet airliners being targeted at long-haul operations.

SNCASE had, in the 1940s, developed the SE-2010 Armagnac, a heavy four-engine piston airliner which did not see commercial success, but led the company to hone its skills in passenger aircraft. It set its designers to producing a concept for the government brief, with various designs ranging from the X-200 to the X-210, which was ultimately submitted for consideration.

This aircraft featured three jet Atar engines clustered around the rear of the fuselage and tail and met the other requirements. It was chosen as a contender, but the committee in charge of choosing a manufacturer asked if SNCASE could instead reduce the number of engines. Thanks to the new Rolls-Royce Avon, which offered additional thrust over the Atar, the manufacturer was able to modify its design by deleting the third engine located in the tail (like the later Trident and Boeing 727). This design was successful and chosen for development in October 1952. Before work commenced, the aircraft was re-designated the SE-210.

Development

After receiving the go-ahead for the Caravelle, SNCASE began a more thorough period of design and perfecting the specifications of the new aircraft. The manufacturer had a set of requirements to ensure were part of their design and had a wish list of items that were increasingly expected of aircraft of the day, such as fail-safe principles where any component or system would have a backup, and not put the aircraft in danger should it fail. This included electrical systems, fuel systems, cockpit design, and even engines; the aircraft would be required to operate safely if one failed.

The Caravelle was one of the handful of early jet airliners to follow the de Havilland Comet, which had entered service in 1952. Peers included the Avro Canada C102 Jetliner and the Tupolev Tu-104, which were in development at the same time as the French jet. Throughout the development period, the Comet was experiencing a number of hull losses, including fatal accidents, which were drawing attention to jet airliner technology and SNCASE was keen to learn from these mistakes and prevent a repeat in their own aircraft. As such, there was cooperation with de Havilland who shared their experiences particularly around fatigue testing, and cockpit design. In fact, the cockpit of the Caravelle is almost identical to the Comet in both external appearance and interior layout, which enabled SNCASE to drastically cut the manufacturing time, and also offer airlines an aircraft which pilots familiar with the Comet could quickly adapt to.

The prototype Caravelle was completed in December 1954, being presented to the world in April of 1955, bearing the test registration F-WHHH. It flew for the first time on 27 May 1955, from Toulouse Blagnac, taking to the skies for a little over 40 minutes where essential handling and systems were tested. Thus followed an extensive testing programme, joined by F-WHHI in May 1956, where tweaks and modifications could be made, and the performance of the jet proved. In fact, during this period the aircraft was presented to various airlines, like first customer Air France, and even operated whole flights on one engine.

As a sign of how European manufacturer Airbus would operate in the future, SNCASE elected to build sections and parts for the Caravelle at various factories across France, being brought together for final assembly in Toulouse.

Early Orders

Air France had committed to an order for 12 Caravelles February 1956, with options for 12 more. The new airliner matched their needs for a domestic and regional aircraft and, despite competition from overseas manufacturers, there was always an expectation in this era that national carriers order home-grown products.

Initially sales were slow; many airlines were fearful of what had been happening with the Comet crashes, and also wooed by the new Boeing and Douglas jets from America. While the prototypes had been presented to most European carriers and displayed at the Paris Air Salon, it was felt a tour of North and South America could attract further sales. VARIG of Brazil was one such airline which made an order, and later both United Airlines and TWA made orders.

Back in Europe, SAS committed to six aircraft with 12 options in June 1957, and at this time production of the airliner began.

Certification of the Caravelle was received by the Secretariat General for Civil and Commercial Aviation (SGACC) on 2 April, 1959. Both F-BHRA and F-BHRB were delivered to Air France that month.

▲ The typical passenger cabin of the Caravelle allowed for a two-three seating configuration with a single aisle. Curtains were still in fashion in airliners of the day and were a feature in the Caravelle aircraft used by many carriers. Overhead hat racks were provided, with later models modified to include lockers with doors. **Dirk Grothe**

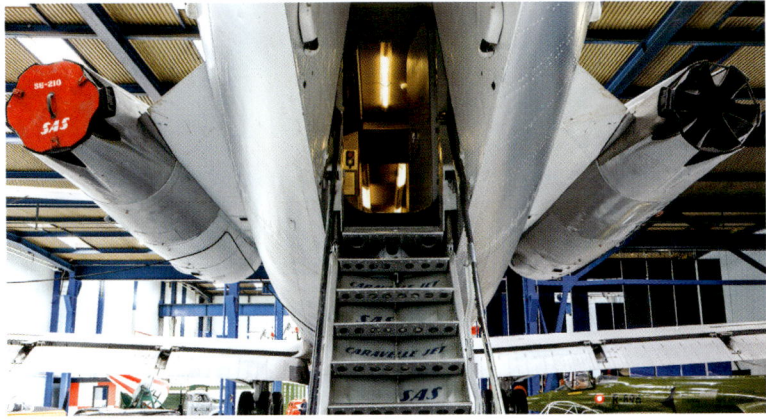

▲ An interesting feature of the Caravelle was a retractable staircase integrated into the rear fuselage, allowing direct access into the cabin. This feature gave the airliner a certain amount of self-sufficiency at airports without airstairs, and became a common feature on some other T-tail airliners developed after the Caravelle, like the Boeing 727, Douglas DC-9 and British Aircraft Corporation One-Eleven. **Dirk Grothe**

Caravelle Variants and Powerplants

F-BHRM was the 37th Caravelle built – a III variant, which spent its entire life flying on the domestic and regional network of Air France. Seen here at London Heathrow in 1976, it was retired three years later.

Caravelle I

The initial model was the Caravelle I, comprising the prototypes and early deliveries to Air France, Air Algerie, SAS and VARIG. These were powered by Rolls-Royce RA-26 Avon Mk 522 engines.

This initial variant was the base model for future Caravelles and included capacity for up to 80 passengers.

Caravelle IA

An upgrade to the Avon engines was developed by Rolls-Royce whereby thrust was increased and noise levels reduced, as well as offering strengthened casing and improved cooling. This was the Avon Mk 522A. Aircraft with this engine were designated Caravelle IA, and entered service in February 1960 with Finnair, who had ordered three examples.

Caravelle III

The Caravelle III actually emerged before the IA, in December 1959, on the 19th aircraft built. It was essentially identical in every way to the original variant but incorporated some modifications to the fuselage. Most notably, it used the further uprated Avon Mk 527 which offered 5,300kg/11,700lb of thrust. This offered airlines a much better take-off performance and allowed a greater take-off weight and range (thanks to an additional fuel tank).

The new model spurred a number of additional airlines to commit to orders, as well as seeing repeat orders from existing carriers. Later, all existing Caravelle I and IA aircraft were converted to III standard.

Caravelle VI-N and VI-R

Further improvements of the Rolls-Royce Avon engines led to plans for Caravelle IV and V models, but these were ultimately dropped when the engines were withheld from production.

The desire to land a noteworthy order from an American carrier saw Sud-Aviation (as SNCASE had now been renamed) work on various modifications to satisfy the requirements of United Airlines. There were also requirements of the Federal Aviation Administration (FAA) to meet if the aircraft was to be certified and sold there. The result was the VI, or 6, models.

With new Avon Mk 531 engines, the first was the VI-N – the letter denoting noise-suppression. The second was the VI-R, designed for United Airlines, and featuring the Mk 533R engine. The 533 included thrust-reversers, meaning the parachute was no longer a requirement.

The United order for 20 aircraft, plus 20 options, was a significant deal for Sud Aviation and France, and represented the first time and American airline had purchased jets from a European manufacturer.

In Europe, the VI-N was delivered to new customer Sabena in February 1961, with the first United VI-R jet following in May.

Caravelle 7 and 8

Two new variants were proposed in the early 1960s, following a collaboration with General Electric to develop new by-pass engines similar to those used on the new Convair 880 airliner. One Caravelle was sent to America for conversion and testing, designated the 7A, although not officially becoming such a variant.

Other models, such as the 7AN and 8 were proposed, and an agreement was signed with the Douglas Aircraft Company to work together on technical development, with Douglas acting as worldwide sales agent for the Caravelle. An order for 20 Caravelle 7As by TWA was received thanks to this arrangement, but later cancelled.

Caravelle 10A

Until this time, all of the Caravelle variants had utilised the same basic fuselage size and shape, with a capacity for up to 80 passengers. However, in 1962 a new stretched model was produced, with capacity for an extra ten passengers thanks to a 1m/3ft extension in front of the wing. It utilised the General Electric CJ.805-23D engines proposed for the 7A, and incorporated improvements to the wing such as double-slotted flaps and modifications to the tail to compensate for the extra fuselage length.

The design was largely to the specification of TWA. One prototype was produced and flown, but no orders received.

Caravelle 10B

Out of the ashes of the failed 10A, Sud Aviation developed the 10B, or 10B3, model. This saw a move to Pratt & Whitney and their JT8D-1 engines, and incorporated the other changes seen in the 10A, such as the fuselage stretch (and increased capacity), and the structural modifications.

The first prototype of this model flew in March 1964, and deliveries started with Finnair and OH-LSA in July once certified. It had a capacity of up to 105 passengers.

The JT8D-7, and -9 engines were latterly made available with this variant, either in production or retrofitted, which offered weight savings and thrust improvements.

Caravelle 10R

The 10R was introduced in 1965 when the prototype flew in January, followed by a first delivery to Alia in May. This model was based on the VI fuselage, with the lower capacity, but offered the Pratt & Whitney engines used on the 10B, and thus the thrust improvements.

The lighting on this photograph of Aero Lloyd Caravelle 10R, D-ABAK, clearly shows the strengthened portion of fuselage where the engines are attached.

Caravelle 11R

The 11R variant was introduced in 1966 and designed to take advantage in the growing market for cargo and freighter aircraft.

It was based on the 10R but included a 93cm/3ft stretch of the fuselage and a cargo door on the port side. This allowed the aircraft to carry up to six standard-sized pallets, or could be configured to carry passengers or a mixture of both in a typical 'combi' mode. It required a strengthened floor, and for the first time included an auxiliary power unit to provide ground power. Only six examples were built, however.

Caravelle 12

The final Caravelle models to be developed came at the end of the 1960s. With requests from a number of airlines for a larger model able to cope with a growing air transport market and the burgeoning inclusive tour industry, Sud Aviation (which at the same time was merging with Nord-Aviation to become SNIAS), developed the 12 variant.

With further stretches over the 10B – 2m/6ft6" forward of the wing, and 1.21m/4ft behind – it created an airliner capable of carrying up to 128 passengers in a single configuration. Other necessary changes came with it, including additional emergency exits, strengthened fuselage and improved ventilation, as well as the latest all-weather landing system. It also utilised the JT8D-9 engines which were the most capable for the extra weight to be carried.

Customers included Air Inter and Sterling, who acquired their own '12B' model with extra range to allow it to link Denmark with the Mediterranean carrying a full load.

The Caravelle 12 entered service in March 1971. However, two years later cracks were discovered in the wings of some examples which led to a temporary grounding and subsequent limitation of service until each airframe could be modified. This somewhat subdued interest in the aircraft, and with greater competition from the likes of Boeing and Douglas, no further Caravelle models were produced. The last airframe, number 280, was delivered to Air Inter on 8 March 1973.

Europe

Europe was naturally the first target for sales of the Caravelle, and the new airliner was designed in cooperation with Air France. The national carrier was expected to place an order for the type, and it did in early 1956, followed shortly after by Scandinavian Airlines System (SAS).

F-BHRH was a built as a Caravelle I in 1959 and was modified into a Caravelle III with improved engines in 1961. It spent its entire life with Air France. It is seen here at London Heathrow, which was a common destination for the French carrier's aircraft on the busy Paris-London link.

German charter operator Aero Lloyd began flying the Caravelle in February 1980 with the acquisition of three second hand 10R models, all previously flown by Aviaco and Iberia. These two shots show D-ACVK, the 176th Caravelle built, in 1985.

Transswede Airways was one of a number of European airlines to take on Caravelles which were being retired from mainline carriers during the 1980s and using them on leisure and charter services. This example, SE-DEH, flew with the airline from 1985 to 1990, and had previously flown for Finnair and Altair.

Transswede's operations covered most of Europe, linking Swedish cities with sun and ski resorts. It later acquired McDonnell Douglas MD-80s and Boeing 737s before being sold to Braathens SAFE in 1997.

Air Enterprise International was a short-lived charter carrier from France which leased this Caravelle 10B3 from Europe Aero Service between 1991 and 1994. Originally built for Finnair as OH-LSE, it spent over a decade with various small French carriers before ending service in Colombia as HK-3955X.

Little is known about Eureka Aviation other than it flew three late-build Caravelle 11R aircraft briefly in the late 1990s. All three wore French test registrations, beginning F-Wxxx, and all had previously flown with the French Air Force. This example, F-WQCT, went on to fly in Africa until 2004.

Aeroflot, the national carrier of the USSR and later Russia was never persuaded to buy the Caravelle, preferring to utilise home-grown types produced by Ilyushin and Tupolev. However, this rare shot captures the time when a Caravelle did spot the colours of the Soviet carrier. F-BJTR, a former Air France Caravelle III, was retired to the Musee de l'Air et de l'Espace at Paris Le Bourget in 1980. It was hired for the 1982 movie "Enigma" to act as an Aeroflot aircraft and thus painted in its livery.

Other Caravelle aircraft were painted in fictitious airline liveries at Le Bourget to act as movie props, including the colours of Air Canada and Interflug.
C Magin

A stunning image of Aerotour Caravelle VI-N in 1980, shortly after the aircraft joined the French leisure carrier from previous owner JAT Yugoslav Airlines. Sadly the airline ceased flying the same year.

Quite a rare shot showing Caravelle III F-BUFH wearing the partial livery of previous owner Sobelair, and the titles of leisure carrier Türkol, in 1981. In fact, the aircraft had recently enjoyed stints flying for Catair and Aerotour, before these titles were applied. However, this was never to be and the aircraft did not enter service with the Turkish airline, instead being sold to Inter-Fret of Ghana.

Orly airport in Paris was the place to see Caravelles. As well as the national carrier Air France, which flew the aircraft on its widespread domestic network, other French airlines would also use it on flights into the airport. This Air Toulouse example, a Caravelle 10B with registration F-GHKM, gives away its true owners as Denmark's Sterling Airways, with the familiar red cheatline and hastily applied stickers on the upper fuselage. It was leased to the French carrier in 1991.

YU-AHK joined JAT Yugoslav Airlines in June 1969. It is one of seven Caravelle VI-Ns ordered by the airline for use on its European and regional services. Most flew with the airline until the late 1970s, however this example was sold to Aerospatiale in 1973, who leased it to Indian Airlines at VT-ECI.

Finnair was an early customer for the Caravelle, taking three IA/3 variants in 1960. This was followed up with an order for ten larger 10B3 models, which started arriving in 1964. This example is OH-LSC, which joined the fleet in August that year and is seen landing in 1975.

Another view of OH-LSC in 1975. These 10B3 variants replaced the original Caravelle IIIs taken on by the airline, and remained in service until sold on in 1981.

Alitalia followed up their initial order for four Caravelle IIIs with a much larger fleet of 17 VI-Ns. It later converted the IIIs into this upgraded model. These aircraft became the mainstay of the airline's domestic and short-haul network, and were eventually replaced by the Douglas DC-9 and Boeing 727 in the 1970s. This particular aircraft lives on in a semi-derelict state close to Entebbe Airport in Uganda.

While the aircraft's registration may be obscured, the helpful construction number and Caravelle variant applied to the lower tailfin confirms the identity as F-BUZC. Once N1009U of United Airlines, this aircraft later flew for Sterling Airways before joining Minerve in 1975. A total of six Caravelles were acquired by this French leisure carrier, being replaced by 1987.

A common scene at northern European airports like Manchester was the Caravelles of Spanish airline Hispania. This charter carrier began life in 1982 using two ageing 10R variants, of which one is seen here.

Already approaching twenty years old in the case of this aircraft, EC-DCN, the reliable Caravelle allowed Hispania to establish itself in the market, but would soon be replaced by more modern types like the Boeing 737. **Kevin Cobb**

Prior to joining Hispania, Caravelle EC-CYI spent seven years on lease to Transeuropa. In fact, this Spanish airline had eight Caravelles pass through its fleet in total, using 11R variants on freight services. The airline eventually folded in 1982.

Swiss air-taxi operator Société Anonyme de Transport Aérien, or SATA for short, decided to expand its business into the inclusive tour charter scene in 1970. Various Caravelle VI-R and 10R models were leased as they were retired by other carriers, including this former Luxair example. Sadly, the crash of a SATA Caravelle in Madeira in 1977 led to financial difficulties for the airline, which closed down a year later.

Only 20 Caravelle 10R models were built. They featured an increased maximum take-off weight thanks to the increased power of its engines, which gave holiday airlines like Aero Lloyd extra lift on those important package holiday flights. Here is D-ACVK, which started life with Iberia in 1966.

Air Charter International leased this Caravelle 10B3 from Europe Aero Service between 1981 and 1990 for holiday flights out of France's regional airports. A sister ship can be seen in the background.

It was perhaps wise to shorten Trabajos Aéreos y Enlaces to TAE to make life easier for non-Spanish holidaymakers flying on this charter airline to sunny destinations in the early days of the package holiday.

Clearly retaining the red cheatline and tail of its true owner, Sterling Airways, TAE leased EC-CUM for four years starting in 1976.

The leisure airline subsidiary of Belgium's Sabena shared many aspects with its parent, including its livery and its fleet. This Caravelle VI-N was leased from Sabena throughout the 1970s. Aside from the titles, it is identical to Sabena and their own Caravelle fleet.

One of the most hardworking and inventive French airlines, Corse Air International, as it was originally known, began life in 1981 with a small fleet of ageing Caravelle VI-Ns that had seen plenty of service already.

Changing its name to Corsair in 1990, the airline is now affiliated with the TUI Group, and is known for having operated a huge fleet of Boeing 747s of every variant except the -8.

Istanbul Airlines was a former Turkish leisure carrier whose Caravelles and later types like the Boeing 737 and 757, could be seen flying in particular to Germany where a large Turkish population resides. TC-ARI is seen at Frankfurt International in 1987.

Another Istanbul Airlines machine. TC-AKA was delivered new to LTU in 1968 and later flew for SAT and Germania, ending its days leased to this Turkish operator.

The Caravelle was the first jet aircraft to be operated by LTU, a German leisure airline founded in 1955. Between 1965 and 1979, seven Caravelle IIIs and 10Rs were flown by the airline, ferrying many passengers to and from their vacations in the sun.

Basking in the Rimini sunshine, Sterling 'Sky Jet' Caravelle 10B3 awaits passengers returning to the colder climes of Denmark in this 1989 shot of the classic jet liner in its later life.

Air Inter had a long association with the Caravelle. It introduced the III variant from 1966 and grew to a fleet of 18 examples, later adding the 12 and some leased VI models. This aircraft, F-BNKD, arrived in February 1967 and is seen at a rainy Paris Orly in 1974.

Transavia Holland's move into the jet age centred around the Caravelle. It initially leased two Caravelle IIIs, and later added many second-hand VI-N and VI-R models, like PH-TRX which began life with United Airlines as N1007U in 1961.

PH-TRH (inset) was another former United Airlines machine, seen here powering away from Amsterdam Schiphol in the early 1970s.

Joining Air France in December 1960, F-BHRY was one of the many Caravelle IIIs flown by Air France – the largest operator of the SE.210. Also in this shot are British Aircraft Corporation One-Eleven and Douglas DC-9 aircraft, which were both influenced by the Caravelle's innovative rear-engine and T-tail design.

LX-LGG rests on a remote stand at Luxembourg Findel airport in 1973. Although popular, the Caravelle was replaced in Luxair's fleet by Boeing 737-200 aircraft in 1978. The modern Boeing jets had greater capacity and more up-to-date avionics and economics.

The Caravelle became Luxair's short-haul jet of choice through the 1970s, with three VI-R models operated through the decade, including LX-LGF seen (inset) at London Heathrow.

Some clarification is needed over the ownership of this aircraft given the various titles visible. Seen in the mid-1970s, F-BJTG wears a basic Air France livery and titles on the engines, with main Air Charter International titles and tail logo. ACI was in fact a subsidiary of Air France and leased this aircraft from them between 1970-83 to fly leisure flights.

Europe Aero Service bought this Caravelle 10B3 from Syrianair in 1982. It was previously YK-AFC, and became F-GDJU. It is captured in 1986 on approach to a cloudy Paris Orly.

Societe de Transports Aeriens Internationaux et Regionaux, or STAIR, was a short-lived French airline which flew this Caravelle 10B3 between 1990 and the airline's demise in 1992. It had previously flown for Finnair, Altair and Transwede, and later flew in Colombia.

Air Service Nantes was another small French carrier to fly the Caravelle. This 10B example joined the fleet in 1988, and flew devoid of titles since the airline often flew on behalf of other carriers. The airline closed down in 1992.

Wearing the later colours of Air Charter (having dropped the 'International') is Caravelle 10B3 F-BJEN. Note the EAS logo underneath the cockpit indicating the owner of this aircraft, which had leased it to Air Charter.

Another view of F-BJEN. The port side has a smaller EAS logo, and 'Super 10' titles. After returning to Europe Aero Service in 1991, the aircraft remained active until 1996 when retired. Today, the forward fuselage is preserved as an aero club office at the tiny Corlier Altiport in the French Alps.

Sterling of Denmark found itself growing just at the right time to be attracted to the possibilities of the Caravelle. Having flown piston airliners like the Douglas DC-6, the Caravelle was the ideal option for taking the airline into the jet age. These were used on the airline's European, Middle Eastern and even North American charter work, with the Caravelle flying non-stop between Oslo and Canada on numerous occasions.

Having initially opted for the Caravelle 10B3, as in the previous picture, Sterling worked with Sud Aviation on developing the larger 12 variant. Seen here is OY-SAC. Seven of the variant, officially called the 12B thanks to its modified take-off weight, were used.

Air Inter retained its early Caravelle IIIs for almost twenty years. This example, F-BNKJ, arrived in 1968 and was retired in 1983. It's seen here at Paris Orly in 1981 sporting the airline's final livery.

Air Toulouse International was a charter carrier founded in 1969, and eventually closing down in 2003 having been rebranded Aeris. During the late 1980s and 90s it flew various Caravelle 10B3 aircraft, like F-GDJU seen here in 1989.

This aircraft, F-GHMU, was flown by Air Toulouse International in its final years and can now be seen preserved at Les Ailes Anciennes museum at Blagnac airport.

The familiarity with the Caravelle in France led to many startup airlines acquiring older airframes in the 1980s and 90s to operate charter services. Aero France International was another such airline, lasting a year or two with this 10B3 F-BJTU, previously of Finnair and Europe Aero Service.

The first of Air Inter's five Caravelle 12 aircraft, F-BTOA, seen at Nice in 1992 very shortly before it was retired from service. The extra capacity of this model was a useful gap for Air Inter between its smaller III variants, and larger Dassault Mercure and Airbus A300 aircraft.

Another of Europe Aero Service's fleet. EAS had wanted to procure Boeing 727s or 737s but was blocked by the French government and so instead turned to acquiring second hand Caravelles. This aircraft, F-GBMJ, is one of a number which previously flew in Argentina and came to France in early 1979.

Aero Jet purchased the assets of defunct Air City in 1992, including this Caravelle 10B3, HB-ICJ. Aero Jet would itself enter bankruptcy in 1996 after failing to establish a viable business amid strong competition. This aircraft moved on to Congo.

TAP Air Portugal operated a modest fleet of only four Caravelle VI-R aircraft, three of which arrived in 1962, including CS-TCC seen here. As the airline modified its operations in the mid-1970s and looked to other types, the Caravelles were sold on.

Always one to draw the attention from enthusiasts, one spotter is caught capturing this Transavia Holland Caravelle III – a very early example, in fact – at Glasgow Airport in 1969.

F-BNKB, a Caravelle III, in active duty with Air Inter at a sunny London Heathrow in 1975. It had flown for the airline since almost new in 1966, despite being ordered and initially delivered to Air France. The national airline actually had a 25% stake in Air Inter and would later merge with the airline in 1997.

The aircraft from the previous picture in later life. Altair was an Italian airline which began flying in 1980, having acquired a small fleet of Caravelle IIIs from Air Inter. The previously owner is clearly evident in this picture of F-GISE seen in 1984.

This aircraft is still in Italy today, preserved as a restaurant in the small town of Sant'Egidio alla Vibrata near the east coast.

Unlike the former Air Inter aircraft acquired by Altair in the previous picture, this aircraft which formerly flew for Finnair, has received its own livery upon joining the Italian airline. This 10B3 variant moved on to Europe Aero Service and Air City a few years later.

Looking somewhat frosty at Dusseldorf is Aero Lloyd's Caravelle 10R D-AAST, which was no doubt about to fly somewhere significantly warmer.

The same aircraft in warmer days at Dusseldorf in 1990. This aircraft would be retired in 1991, but the cockpit is reportedly still in Germany as a private simulator.

Finnair's Caravelle 10B OH-LSF flew with the airline from 1966 until 1985, with a brief spell on loan to Altair as I-GISI in 1984. The Finnish national carrier used its fleet of ten Caravelle 10s on most of its European network and they were a common sight until replaced by Douglas DC-9s and the larger MD-80 family.

Union de Transports Aériens, or UTA, had possibly the most widespread worldwide coverage with its Caravelle fleet, despite only operating four examples. The French carrier took delivery of two 10R models in 1966 and 67 respectively, with a 10B3 leased briefly in the same period. A Caravelle III was also leased in late 1971. These aircraft were used both on African flights out of Paris Le Bourget (via intermediate stops), and also from the airline's outpost at Noumea in New Caledonia, where they flew to other French territories in the Pacific, as well as New Zealand.

Transavia Holland's PH-TRH seen taxying onto stand at Ibiza in 1971 ready to despatch another 80 passengers on their vacation, and take another 80 home.

Air Inter's F-BNKB powers out of London Heathrow in 1975 heading for Paris. It was operating a flight on behalf of Air France, which also used its own Caravelles on the route.

Swissair was an early Caravelle III operator, but acquired its aircraft through a business cooperation with SAS. The Scandinavian carrier leased one aircraft in early 1960, and then ordered another three for the Swiss airline, including HB-ICX seen here at Zurich. In total nine examples were flown by Swissair until the early 1970s when the Douglas DC-9 was introduced. The aircraft seen here was sold to Catair, then China Airlines.

Belgian International Air Services, or BIAS, was a little-known airline which existed between 1959 and 1980. It operated a mixed fleet of types, from small commuter airliners up to the Douglas DC-8, and these were flown on charter services, as well as some scheduled flights. In 1971 single Caravelle VI-R was bought from United Airlines, seen here, and operated for a year or two.

This Caravelle 10B3 appears to have two identities. It wears the full livery of Corse Air International, a French charter airline, while the aircraft's registration is that of African nation Mali. In fact, this aircraft was owned by Air Mali and spent six months on lease to the French carrier, who later bought it and gave it the registration F-GEPC.

Originally built for Air France, this Caravelle III spent its career flying for the French Air Force on transport and VIP duties. It had the military serial 141, and the civilian registration F-RAFG. Once its active duties were over, the aircraft was donated to the Musee de l'Air et de l'Espace at Paris Le Bourget, where it is under restoration. **Jean Nalfer**

Another view of TAE's Caravelle 10B3 EC-CUM seen at Newcastle Airport ready to take another load of holidaymakers to the Spanish sun. This variant of the Caravelle featured a stretch over the VI models, and could carry 105 passengers, which made it attractive to charter carriers.

A classic scene of the 1970s showing the Caravelle hard at work in France. With an Air France Boeing 727 just visible behind, this Air Inter machine is offloading its passengers via the forward and integral rear stairs onto a hot airport apron.

Seen at what is likely to be Prague airport, this scene of classic jets features an Ilyushin Il-62 and Tupolev Tu-134 of CSA Československé Airlines with a Finnair Caravelle 10B3 in the centre. This picture was taken in 1981, which was the final year Finnair flew this aircraft.

Swiss charter airline Air City started Caravelle operations in 1988 but was ultimately unsuccessful amid competition from bigger carriers. Its livery was nevertheless striking and showed off the Caravelle's lines well.

Yet another livery worn by Altair's Caravelles. This smart scheme or reds and blacks adorns I-GISA, a Caravelle III bought by Finnair in 1960 and by the time of this shot over twenty years old. The short lived airline's fleet of jets were sold on in 1984, with this aircraft finding its way to IAC Airlines in Congo Kinshasa, as it was then known.

Special Air Transport, or SAT, was founded in 1978 to fly charter and holiday flights out of Cologne and Düsseldorf. It acquired this single Caravelle 10R from fellow German leisure airline LTU in 1978, followed by two more the next year. The airline was renamed Germania in 1986, and the Caravelles continued on under this new identity. **Dirk Grothe**

Air Provence was an all-rounder, with specialisms in different fields of air travel from medical flights to freight and passenger charters. Its fleet ranges from single engine pistons through executive jets and large airliners like the Caravelle 12. In fact, the airline had the prestige of becoming the last European operator of the Caravelle in passenger service when it retired these jets in 1996.

North America

The first of United's Caravelles entered service on French national day, 14 July, 1961 serving the key New York to Chicago route. This gave United a competitive edge by introducing jets on the route versus the propliners of their rivals.

Unfortunately, the arrival of the Boeing 727 and 737 in the mid- and late-1960s meant the smaller Caravelle lost its appeal and follow-up orders were not placed. United retired its entire fleet by March 1972.

Airborne Express was one of the great names in America's freight airline business. It was founded in 1946 and grew into a large carrier based out of its Wilmington, OH hub. The name Airborne Express was only adopted in 1980 following the airline's merger with Midwest Air Charter.

A small fleet of Caravelles were acquired as package freighters and transferred across to Airborne Express with the merger. They initially wore Midwest / Airborne Charter Express titles, as in this shot of N903MW.

Later, the titles were standardised simply to Airborne Express.

This was one of only two major airlines to fly the Caravelle in the United States (the other being United Airlines), and the only one to fly the type as a freighter in the country. The aircraft were retired in 1984, with this aircraft, N907MW, being used for many years as a training aid at Cincinnati airport.

South America

Originally built for Finnair and delivered in 1967, this Caravelle 10B3 later spent time flying with Europe Aero Service and Air Charter in France, and even briefly on lease to ZAS Airlines of Egypt. In 1993 it was sold to Colombia, flying with this airline known as SEC or SERCA. It was seized in Mexico in 1995 for alleged drug smuggling activities, and spent its final years flying with the Mexican Air Force.

Interestingly, today this airframe is one of two Caravelles preserved at the Parque Aviacuatico Los Manantiales some 165km north wet of Mexico City.

The other Caravelle airframe preserved at the Parque Aviacuatico Los Manantiales in Mexico is this 10R example. Seen here flying for Colombian cargo carrier Aerosucre, which flew Caravelles from the early 1980s.

This particular aircraft began life with Iberia as EC-BIF, and later flew for Aero Lloyd. Like the aircraft in the previous picture, it was seized by the Mexican government in 1994 while flying for Aerogolfo Colombia.

Aerotal was a domestic and regional airline founded in Colombia in 1970. It grew to become an important presence in the country's aviation scene, flying Douglas DC-3 and DC-4 piston airliners. This Caravelle 6R was acquired from LAN Chile in 1975 to operate on busier and more prestigious routes until it was replaced by Boeing 727s. The airline ceased flying in 1983.

HC-BAJ was a 1962-vintage Caravelle 6R built for TAP Air Portugal. It was sold to Servicios Aereos Nacionales, or SAN Ecuador, in 1975. It was one of three aircraft purchased from the Portuguese carrier to operate on the busy Quito to Guayaquil route, however one of the aircraft was used as a source of spare parts. Two others were purchased from Luxair, and the type remained with the airline until 1986. SAN later operated Boeing 727s, and merged with SAETA in 1990. The airline closed down in 1999.

VIASA was the national carrier of Venezuela until 1997 and operated a broad range of different aircraft types. In the late 1960s the airline was adding Douglas DC-8 and DC-9 jet types to its fleet, but it also leased this Caravelle 3, YV-C-AVI, from AVENSA, another Venezuelan carrier, between 1969-70. The aircraft had started life with Air Algerie in 1960, and was sadly written off in an accident at Barquismento in 1973.

Indian Airlines began its affiliation with the Caravelle in December 1963 with this aircraft, VT-DPN, and stablemate VT-DPO. In all, some 12 Caravelle VI-N models were operated by the airline before the final example was removed from service in 1980. **Jimmy Wadia**

VT-DVI joined the fleet in October 1966. Indian Airlines had a poor reputation with the Caravelle, with five being destroyed in accidents over the course of the type's service. These incidents were put down to poor crew training, airport and weather conditions. They were ultimately replaced by Boeing 737s through the 1970s. **Jimmy Wadia**

Syrian Arab Airlines was an early customer of the Caravelle 10B3 variant when it took delivery of its first example in October 1965. This aircraft, YK-AFD, was part of a follow-up order placed in 1971 to bring the fleet to four examples.

Syrianair, as the airline was later called, added this new livery in the late 1970s. Its Caravelles were used on services from Damascus to European and Middle Eastern destinations, supplementing the Boeing 707 fleet.

Syrianair Caravelle 10B3 YK-AFC seen at Geneva alongside a Boeing 707 of neighbouring Alia from Jordan.

Ultimately, as with the case of many Caravelle operators, Syrianair turned to Boeing for its fleet renewal and acquired three 727s. These would replace the Caravelles by 1971, with YK-AFB seen parked up pending disposal. It was still present at the airport as recently as 2006.

Thai Airways International was founded in 1959 to look at expanding the international operations of its domestic carrier. In 1963 the Caravelle III was chosen as part of its growing fleet, with this example leased from Scandinavian Airlines System (SAS) who were providing assistance to the Asian airline.

In all some 14 Caravelle IIIs were flown by Thai between 1963 and 1970, opening up its network around the Far East.

This aircraft was returned to SAS in 1970, and is seen here at Copenhagen Airport that year, before it was repainted and returned to its Swedish registration of SE-DAE.

Still going strong today as Royal Jordanian Airlines, ALIA was the national carrier of Jordan and acquired three Caravelle 10Rs in 1965. They were used on the airline's European and Middle Eastern network out of Amman, until replaced by Boeing 727s in the mid-1970s.

JY-ACT, seen here, would infamously go on to fly for SATA of Switzerland and crash off the island of Madeira in 1977.

XU-JTB is a Caravelle III originally delivered to Air France in 1961 as F-BJTA. Sold to Air Cambodge in 1973 to replace an earlier example destroyed in a guerrilla attack on Phnom Penh. This aircraft was itself used as a means of escape for President Lon Nol in 1975, and was abandoned at Bangkok Don Mueang airport. It is still thought to exist in the fire training compound. **John Wegg**

Corse Air International acquired this Caravelle 10B3 in 1984 and subsequently leased it to Air Caledonie later the same year. It is seen here in basic Corse Air livery, with small stickers indicating its ownership under the forward windows. The aircraft was later sold to the Pacific-based airline, where it remained until 1990.

Far Eastern Air Transport was a Taiwanese domestic carrier founded in 1957 which quickly became a dominant force in the island nation's air travel industry. As it began to look for replacements for its older turboprop Viscount aircraft, it took on two Caravelle VI-R aircraft in 1973, formerly flown by Iberia. A third was added a year later.

These aircraft operated on the airline's domestic network (and some international services) until retired in the late 1970s. This aircraft, B-2501, was the first to arrive, and is seen here in storage at Taipei Songshan in 1981.

Africa

*Nigeria's Okada Air was known as a purveyor of used, classic airliners. Its fleet included all manner of airliners from the main British, American and other manufacturers from the 1980s until its demise in 1997. This Caravelle VI-N was no exception, joining the airline from Europe Aero Service in 1983 to live out its final years. By the time of this picture, it was already being used as a parts source. **Eddy J Gual***

Caravelle III was donated to the newly rebranded Air Burundi by Air France in 1975. It had previously flown as F-BJTM. By 1976 the aircraft had been converted for freight and VIP duties.

TU-TCO was one of two Caravelle 11Rs delivered to pan-African airline Air Afrique in July 1967. These were the variants with cargo doors enabling an all-cargo or mixed configuration. The airline later added second hand 10R and VI-N models.

Air Alexandrie was a brief sidenote in Egyptian aviation, set up to operate flights between Cairo and Tel Aviv, which could not be flown by the national carrier. Two Caravelle IIIs were acquired for the purpose in 1980, but ultimately would not be used for the service which would be flown by another airline.

This former United Airlines and Sterling Caravelle VI-R was acquired by the Government of Mauritania in 1974 for use a VIP transport. It would see out its days based here.

Royal Air Maroc was an early adopter of the Caravelle, ordering a IA model for delivery in 1960 (which was later upgraded to a III variant). This was supplemented by four more IIIs later in the 1960s, and the airline also leased in aircraft from other carriers.

CN-CCY and -CCZ were the last to leave the fleet, at the end of 1976, when modern Boeing 737-200s were brought in.

An early Caravelle III, built for VARIG as the tenth production example, later found life flying for the heads of state of the Central African Republic as TL-AAI. It was joined by 10R TL-ABB and wore various liveries during this time.

Built in 1965 for SAS, this Caravelle III spent the longest period of its life flying for the Government of Rwanda, between 1974-1992. It flew in VIP configuration but was later sold back into airline service with Trans Zaire Airways.

Although not visible, the registration of this Chadian VIP Caravelle VI-R is TT-AAM, pictured at Paris in 1976 alongside the Mauritanian government example seen previously. Like other examples, it flew heads of state on official business.

Air Mali bought this Caravelle 10B3 from Syrianair in 1980 for services out of Bamako. The same aircraft is seen earlier while on lease to Corse Air, whom it was later sold to in 1984, when Air Mali introduced the Boeing 737.

Air Congo was founded in 1961 and ordered two Caravelle 11Rs in 1967, capable of cargo and passenger operations, with uprated Engines, essential in parts of Africa. The cargo door can clearly be seen on this shot of 9Q-CLD, with passengers using the rear ventral air stairs.

In 1971 Air Congo changed its name to Air Zaire, with very little change in the livery. The airline retained its Caravelles until 1976, when both were sold to the French Air Force, no doubt keen for their cargo capabilities.

One of the early adopters of the Caravelle was Air Algerie, which had close links with France and regular services across the Mediterranean between the two countries. Three IAs were initially taken on in 1959/60, including 7T-VAI, seen here in 1964 after conversion to a III. Later more III and VI-N models were added.

Seen at London Gatwick in 1966, TS-TAR was the second Caravelle delivered to Tunis Air, two years prior. It was a III model, with three others in the fleet and many more leased in temporarily before the airline switched over to the Boeing 727 in the later 1970s.

Two pictures of Caravelle III aircraft with Kabo Air titles, but still wearing the basic identities of their previous owners, namely Air France and Air Inter.

F-BJTE was never flown commercially, becoming a source of spare parts for other aircraft in the fleet. Meanwhile, F-BNKA became 5N-AWF and flew with the Nigerian airline through the 1980s. **Christian Volpati**

A Libyan Arab Airlines Caravelle VI-R, 5A-DAB, on approach to land with its large, single-slotted flaps deployed. Two Caravelles were ordered by Kingdom of Libya Airlines in 1965, with the airline changing its name four years later. It remained with the airline until 1975.

Gabon Express has an important role in the story of the Caravelle, for this African airline which began services in 1988 was the last airline to fly the French jet in passenger service.

This aircraft, a Caravelle 11R, was built in 1967 for Air Congo and spent most of its life in Africa. It was actually sold on to Waltair in 2000, who flew it for a few more years. However, Gabon Express would fly their other Caravelle until 2004.

Caravelle Survivors

Le Caravelle Club was formed by a group of Caravelle enthusiasts with the intention of saving and preserving a former SAS Caravelle III. SE-DAI was delivered in 1966, and in 1971 was sold to the Swedish Air Force for use in a signals intelligence role. It remained active with them until retired in 1998. It was then flown to Stockholm Arlanda, and since then it has been kept 'alive', albeit not flying.

Preserved for over 30 years at Lyon Satolas airport was former Air France Caravelle F-BHRM. It flew with the airline between 1960 and 1979. By 2010 the aircraft's condition had declined, and it has now sadly been scrapped.

The first aircraft in the significant order placed by United Airlines for the Caravelle VI-R was N1001U. It flew with the airline between 1961-71, and was then sold to Aero Service Corp, and then the Western Geophysical Corp. In 1990 the aircraft was retired to the Pima Air & Space Museum in Tucson, AZ. Note the special pod under the fuselage used in aerial mapping surveys.

One of the former Airborne Express Caravelle freighters, used until 1985, found its way to preservation at the Ohio History of Flight Museum, where this picture was taken. Since then, it has become a training aid for the fire service at Columbus International Airport. **Bjorn Spratte**

*Starting life with SAS in 1960, OY-KRD is a Caravelle III which flew with the airline until 1974. Since 1998 it has been on display at the Danmarks Flyvemuseum in Helsingor and is in immaculate condition. The inset image shows it outside the museum, and the second (by **Dirk Grothe**) now on display inside the hall.*

One example of a Caravelle with an interesting post-retirement life is OY-STD, previously with Sterling. Following retirement, the cockpit section was retained for use by Copenhagen Airport as a training aid. It shows signs of various traumas. **Dirk Grothe**

The Aeroscopia museum at Toulouse Blagnac is home to the last Caravelle built. F-BTOE was a Caravelle 12 delivered to Air Inter in 1973 and was finally retired in the early 1990s. This museum is home to many important airframes built at the Toulouse site, particularly from the Airbus stable.

Not far from Aeroscopia at Toulouse is the Les Ailes Anciennes, another museum of important and historic aircraft, both civil and military. Caravelle 10B3 F-GHMU is preserved here in the livery of its final operator, Air Toulouse International. It was delivered new to Sterling in 1968.

The second Caravelle built, and used in the early testing and certification process, was F-WHHI (later registered F-BHHI). It never flew commercially, but became a training aid for Air France, and was eventually dismantled in 1969. The cockpit section was saved and is now on display at the Musee de L'Air et de L'Espace at Paris Le Bourget.